Fountain of Youth

Illustrated by Kathy Kifer, Dahna Solar and Charla Barnard

Published by

Garlic Press

100 Hillview Lane #2
Eugene, OR 97408

ISBN 0-931993-86-5
Order Number GP-086

The **Sign Language Literature Series** presents stories from different cultures. *Fountain of Youth* is a Korean tale of reward and punishment influenced by the Confucian teachings of loyalty and responsibility to family, self-discipline and restraint, and the proper way to relate to others.

The story is presented in simple language, full illustration, and is complemented with illustrated signs.

Long ago, kind old couple without children live mountains.

A long time ago, a kind old couple
without any children lived in the mountains.

Cross selfish old man live next to couple.

A cross and selfish old man
lived next to the couple.

One day

kind old man cut

wood when beautiful bird

lead him bubbling spring.

One day the kind old man was
cutting wood when a beautiful bird
led him to a bubbling spring.

He drink

sweet cold water

from spring fall asleep.

He drank the sweet cold water
from the spring and fell asleep.

When her husband did not return,
the old woman was very worried.

She ask cross old neighbor help search for husband, old man refuse.

The greedy, selfish old neighbor was surprised
when he saw the young couple.

The couple directed the greedy old man
to the spring.

Young couple return spring. Find baby dress like old neighbor.

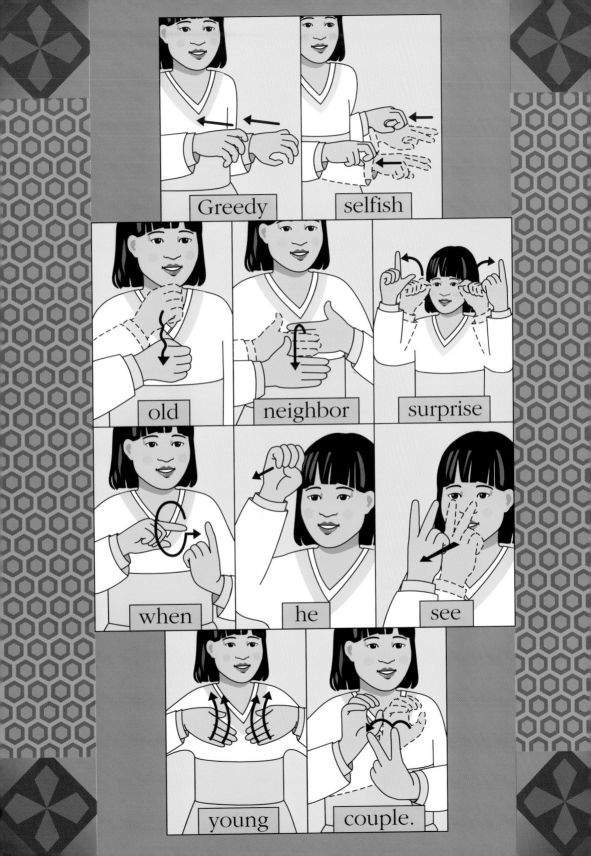

Greedy selfish old neighbor surprise when he see young couple.

He led her to the spring and
she drank the water.

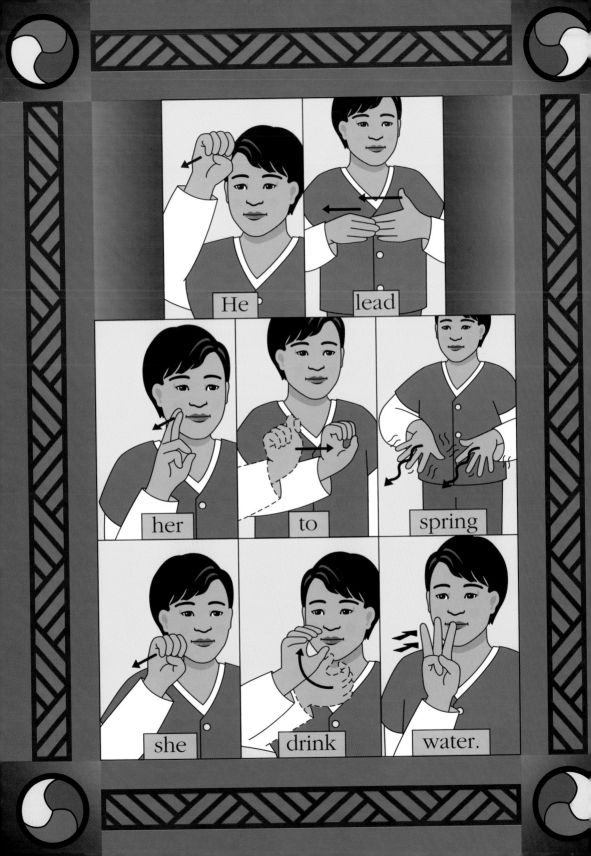

He told her about the bird
and drinking from the bubbling spring.

The old woman heard someone whistling,
"Husband! Is it really you? You're young again!"

She asked the cross old neighbor
to help search for her husband, but he refused.

The young couple returned to the spring
to find a baby dressed like the old neighbor.

Couple adopt baby teach become kind and loving.

The couple adopted the baby
and taught him to be kind and loving.

Other sign language books from Garlic Press

Finger Alphabet GP-046
Uses word games and activities to teach the finger alphabet.

Signing in School GP-047
Presents signs needed in a school setting.

Can I Help? Helping the Hearing Impaired in Emergency Situations GP-057
Signs, sentences and information to help communicate with the hearing impaired.

Caring for Young Children: Signing for Day-Care Providers and Sitters GP-058
Signs for feelings, directions, activities and foods, bedtime, discipline and comfort-giving.

An Alphabet of Animal Signs
GP-065   Animal illustrations and associated signs for each letter of the alphabet.

Mother Goose in Sign GP-066
Fully illustrated nursery rhymes.

Number and Letter Games
GP-072   Presents a variety of games involving the finger alphabet and sign numbers.

Songs in Sign GP-071
Six songs in Signed English. The easy-to-follow illustrations enable you to sign along.

Foods GP-087
A colorful collection of photos with signs for 43 common foods.

Fruits & Vegetables GP-088
Thirty-nine beautiful photos with signs.

Coyote & Bobcat GP-081
A Navajo story serving to tell how Coyote and Bobcat got their shapes.

Raven & Water Monster GP-082
This Haida story tells how Raven gained his beautiful black color and how he brought water to the earth.

Fountain of Youth GP-086
This Korean folk tale about neighbors shows the rewards of kindness and the folly of greed.

Ananse the Spider: Why Spiders Stay on the Ceiling GP-085
A West African folk tale about the boastful spider Ananse and why he now hides in dark corners.